The Old
Basketball

A Story of Compassion

GAIL BOX INGRAM

Illustrated by C. E. Glaze

WestBow Press books may be ordered through booksellers or by contacting:

WestBow Press
A Division of Thomas Nelson & Zondervan
1663 Liberty Drive
Bloomington, IN 47403
www.westbowpress.com
1 (844) 714-3454

Illustrated by C.E. Glaze

ISBN: 978-1-6642-0915-2 (sc)
ISBN: 978-1-6642-0916-9 (e)

Library of Congress Control Number: 2020920328

Print information available on the last page.

WestBow Press rev. date: 11/19/2020

WestBow
PRESS®
A DIVISION OF THOMAS NELSON
& ZONDERVAN

Also by Gail Box Ingram

Komorebi: Light Shining Through

GAIL BOX INGRAM

"Vivid images evoking God's intersection with our lives. These poems bring us needed respite in a world of wounds." **Jane Kirkpatrick**

KOMOREBI
Light Shining Through

I had been placed on the compost pile and forgotten. The sun had faded me and rain had splashed me with mud. I had a dent in my side because I needed some air. I was really sad and lonely, but I could only sit and watch as the boys played with the other balls.

One sunny day I woke up hearing a little boy saying over and over, "Baketbaw, baketbaw, baketbaw." I opened my eyes as the sound came closer. Then I saw the little boy winding his way through the weeds in the garden. He was coming to me! He seemed determined to get **ME,** even though there were other balls under the goal at the edge of the garden.

His mother was following him saying, "Honey, you're gonna get your face scratched. Watch out for the briars...Be careful! That ball's been thrown away. It's old and rough. Look, it's all pushed in." But the little boy kept coming with his arms stretched out, reaching toward me on the compost pile.

At last his mom reached onto the compost bin and lifted me down for the little boy. He was so pleased that he smiled up at his mom while holding me!

Then the little boy made his way back through the maze to the base of the basketball goal holding me happily in his wee hands. I thought, "When he sees I can't bounce, he probably will throw me away again."

But no! He lifted me over his head. Then that little boy did his best to shoot me at the basket! "Doal," he said to his mom.

12

"Yes, that's the goal, William," she said, "Make two!!" She even helped him get me up higher as I left his little raised hands. It felt so good to be sailing through the air toward the goal again.

But, uh-oh, I fell to the pavement with a dull
thud. There I lay after rising about two inches
off the ground. I was surely a goner now.

NO! The little guy started all over again. "Baketbaw, baketbaw," he said, picking me up and walking around under the goal with me in his hands. This made me soooooo happy!

When it was time for the little boy to leave, he left me on the pavement with the other balls. He did not put me back on the compost bin.

The big guys came home from school. They threw me over close to the wood pile. I lay there in the grass till the next time the little boy came to play.

I was so happy to hear his tiny steps on the pavement and his small voice saying, "Baketbaw, baketbaw." He passed by all the better balls. The little boy came straight to me!

I had found a true friend. Now I stay on the pavement with the other balls. My dent is gone, and dirt isn't caked on me anymore. I wait each day for my little friend to come. When he plays with me, I am so happy! Thank you, little boy!

AFTERWORD

Our son was born when I was 43, an answer to prayer for another child. My career was going full swing at the time and I missed a lot of his first year. When he turned one, I went back to hospital shift work. My schedule was weird, but I had all of my mornings with my little son who was now walking. Wellman Drive was a friendly and sharing neighborhood in Donelson, TN. The neighbors were involved in one another's lives: children playing together, piano lessons, block party picnics in summer, caroling at Christmas, sharing food, vegetables and flowers from one another's gardens.

The Egans, across the street from our house, had a real basketball goal in their back yard at the edge of their pavement, their drive coming down the hill making a turnaround at the basement garage. The older boys from the neighborhood congregated in the afternoons after school in this back yard for basketball. Will was about 18 months old and his Dad would carry him over there to watch the big boys play basketball. The next morning, when his Dad was at work, Will would go to the front door or picture window in our home and reach his little hands toward the house across the street saying, "Baketbaw, baketbaw!" He wanted to go play.

This story unfolded on one of our trips to the basketball goal. Little did I know what was waiting there. This story came to me seeing all through the eyes of the old basketball. Compassion for others, the lonely, the downtrodden, those in hard circumstances became such a part of our son's life and it seemed to begin here. He still lives that way as an adult.

Of course the little boy did not know he was showing compassion for the old, dented, dirty ball. But, he did not look on it with scorn or say ugly things to it. He did not bully it. Here it is 28 years after the story was written and, as I was getting ready to self-publish it, I realized this story can be used to model anti-bullying, understanding and acceptance of those different from us, the meaning of wonderful things like compassion, tolerance, kindness and how these help bring peace to our world. I believe these are good things to teach children. The little boy accepted the old basketball with all of its imperfections. This is how God accepts us. Our hearts should smile knowing our Creator loves us always!

From The Passion Translation

"Dedicate your children to God and point them in the way that they should go and the values they've learned from you will be with them for life." **Proverbs 22:6**

"When he saw the vast crowds of people, Jesus' heart was deeply moved with compassion, because they seemed weary and helpless..." **Matthew 9:36**

"Lord, you're so kind and tenderhearted to those who don't deserve it and so patient with people who fail you! Your love is like a flooding river overflowing

EPILOGUE: for Parents and Children

(This page and the Glossary are the Teaching Guide.)

Hello boys and girls. I am the old basketball. Did you like the story about me and my little friend? Please see if you can answer these questions for me. And look at the list of words on page 25. Those words are here as the glossary to tell you what the words mean. So, get ready!! Here are the questions I have for you.

1. Did the little boy accept me just the way I was?
2. How did this make me feel?
3. Did the little boy show compassion for me?
4. Have you ever been kind and compassionate to someone or something different from you?
5. Do you like for others to treat you with kindness?
6. Is being kind to someone showing tolerance to them?
7. Did the little boy bully me?
8. Have you ever been bullied by someone else?
9. Compassion and tolerance help the world be in peace. Do you understand this?
10. Did the little boy forgive the old basketball?
11. What did you learn from reading my story?

GLOSSARY

1. **Accept:** to receive willingly*
2. **Acceptance:** approval *
3. **Bullying:** abuse and mistreatment of someone vulnerable by someone stronger *
4. **Compassion:** sympathetic pity and concern for the sufferings or misfortunes of others**
5. **Compassionate:** feeling or showing sympathy and concern for others**
6. **Compost:** decayed organic material used as a plant fertilizer**
7. **Compost heap, bin or pile:** a container or pile of garden and organic kitchen refuse which decomposes to produce compost**
   Note: The compost heap the old basketball was on was made of wire.
8. **Empathy:** the ability to understand and share the feelings of another**
9. **Forgive:** stop feeling angry or resentful toward someone for an offense, flaw or mistake**
10. **Kindness:** the quality of being friendly, generous, and considerate**
11. **Peace:** freedom from disturbance, tranquility**
12. **Tolerance:** the act of allowing something*
13. **Tolerate:** to put up with*

The definitions above were chosen with younger children in mind. Therefore two separate dictionaries were used.

* Merriam Webster Dictionary Online

** Oxford Languages Dictionary Online

Citations:

"all definitions marked by one asterisk*." *Merriam-Webster.com*. 2020. https://www.merriam-webster.com (19 September2020)

"all definitions marked with two asterisks**." *Oxford English Dictionary. com.2020*. https://languages.oup.com/research/oxford-english-dictionary/ (19 September 2020)

ACKNOWLEDGEMENTS and DEDICATION

Thank you to Will, the little boy with the compassionate heart, and his Heavenly Father who made him the way he is and who showed me this story. Thank you for all the neighbors on Wellman Drive who made it such a great place to live and raise children, for parents all over the world, especially America and Japan, who are teaching their children to be compassionate, kind and accepting individuals, pointing them to bringing peace to our world; for our nieces Kelli Burbage, Kim Kalinauskas, and Katie Griffies, our daughter Carrie Suenaga, our son Will Ingram, my friends Janice Garey and Sarah Aghedo, all writers, artists, and teachers in their own world, who proofed and discussed this book with me. To my friend and illustrator, C.E. Glaze, without whom the book would not be finished yet!

TO LIKE IT ALL

I want to like everything---
Onions, tomatoes, fish---
I want to like them all,
Everything in the meals
My mother makes.
I want to like everyone---
Doctors, crows---
All of them, too.
Everything and everyone in the world
God has made.
--by Misuzu Kaneko, Japanese Poet from Yamaguchi, 1903-1929

Poem from the book **ARE YOU AN ECHO? The Lost Poetry of Misuzu Kaneko**, published in 2016 by Chin Music Press, Seattle, Washington, USA. Used with permission of Sally Ito, the translator of this particular poem.

This book is dedicated to Misuzu Kaneko, an observant and compassionate poet. Her poems are taught in the schools in Japan. Our daughter and her family, the David Satoshi Suenagas, live in Yamaguchi City, Japan.

About the Author

The author and her son Will in June, 2020

Gail Box Ingram was born and raised in Alabama, USA. She lived in Tennessee 30 years after obtaining a BS degree in Medical Technology from David Lipscomb University. She began writing poetry when she was 14 and always loved expressing herself in the written word, being an avid letter writer like her Mother's side of the family! Gail is the mother of two children, both grown now, grandmother of two wonderful Japanese American grandchildren, married to Bracken Ingram, Dad and Daddo (his Grandfather name) for 47 years the year this is published. Her Grandmother name is Nana. The only foreign country she has traveled to is Japan and that for 10 different trips since 2005. It is the only place abroad she has ever wanted to go. She is a lifelong student of God's Word, the Holy Bible, and of realizing what it means to be in Christ. Gail is a compassionate person who has endeavored in life to raise compassionate children and grandchildren. She and Bracken live in the countryside in south central Alabama now, calling their place the Ponderosa, though not owning livestock, just dogs! She returned to Alabama in 2001 to help care for her Mother, who was widowed and had dementia.

Printed in the United States
By Bookmasters